Princess W...
a Play

written by Jay Dale
illustrated by Mélanie Florian

"Mrs Kay," said Princess, "may we put on a play for the mums and dads? We could practise every day after school."

"I'm sorry," said Mrs Kay sadly. "I'm helping to put on the school sports' day over the next four weeks. I will be helping Mr Sanders every day after school."

3

Princess felt sad, too.
She really wanted to put on a play.
She loved to write, and she loved to act.

"Mrs Kay," said Princess,
"I could write the play by myself.
Then everyone in the class
could help to put it on."

"Well," said Mrs Kay,
"let me think it over."

5

The next day,
Princess asked Mrs Kay again.
"Mrs Kay," said Princess,
"may we put on a play?
I can write the play,
and everyone can help
to put it on."

"I will help!" said Dara.
"I will, too," said Bill.
"We will all help," said the children.

Mrs Kay smiled.
"If you all help," she said,
"then you **may** put on a play!"

"Yippee!" shouted the children.
"It will be the best play ever!"

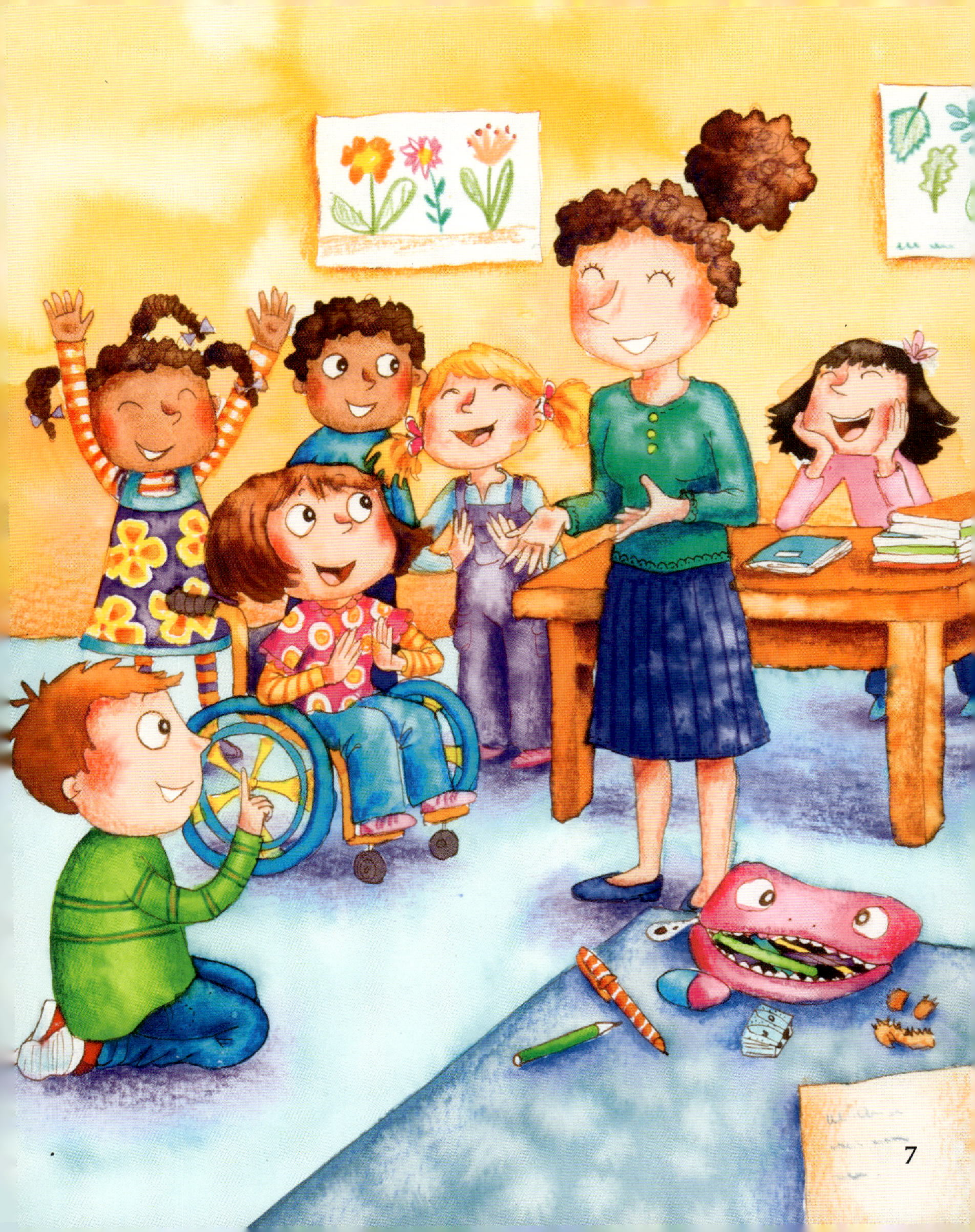

That night when Princess got home,
she went to work.

Tap! Tap! Tap!

She worked on the play before dinner,
and she worked on the play after dinner.

"Princess, you should be in bed,"
said Mum, looking at her watch.

"But, Mum," smiled Princess,
"I can't go to bed just yet.
I have to finish the play!"

Tap! Tap! Tap!

At last, just after 9 o'clock,
Princess stopped writing.
"Yes!" she said quietly to herself.
"The play is finished!"

The next day, Princess gave everyone
a copy of the play.
It was about an old woman
who lived in a big house.
Her garden was so beautiful,
animals from all over
wanted to live there.
All the children in the class
thought it was the best play ever.
And everyone had a part to play.

For three weeks, the children practised
the play every day.
They met in the hall after school
and practised the play over and over.

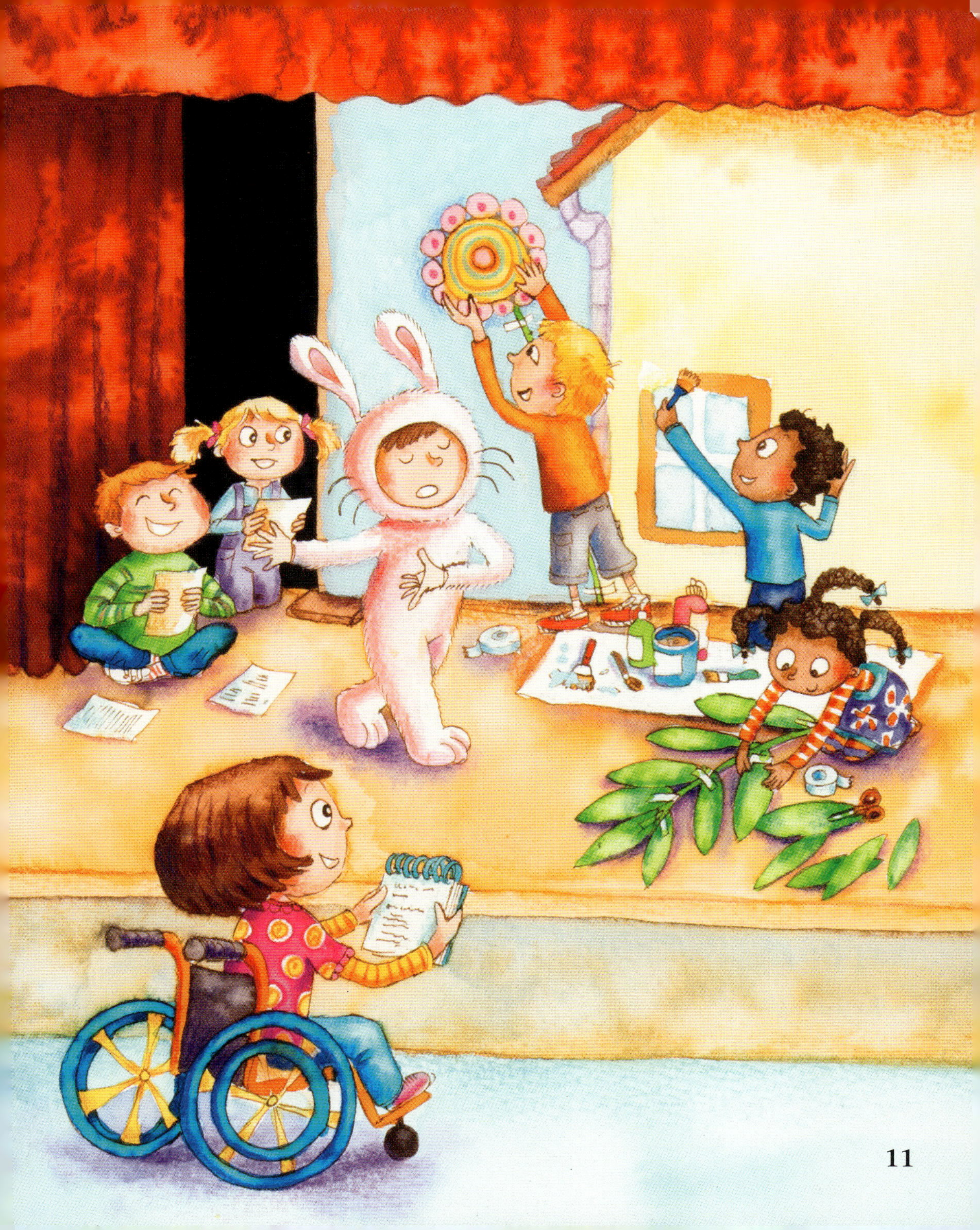

At last, it was time to put on the play
for the mums and dads and their friends.

Princess was the old woman
who lived in the big house.
She looked very funny
in an old pink hat
with a tall green feather.

All the children knew just what to do.
Everyone had learned their words.

13

At the end of the play,
all the mums and dads
clapped and clapped.

Mrs Kay came up onto the stage.
"I'm so happy with all of you,"
she said.
"You have all worked very hard."

At last, it was Bill's turn to say something.
Bill looked over at Princess.
"We all want to thank Princess,"
he said.
"She is the best writer ever.
And one day, Princess will write plays
for people all around the world to see."

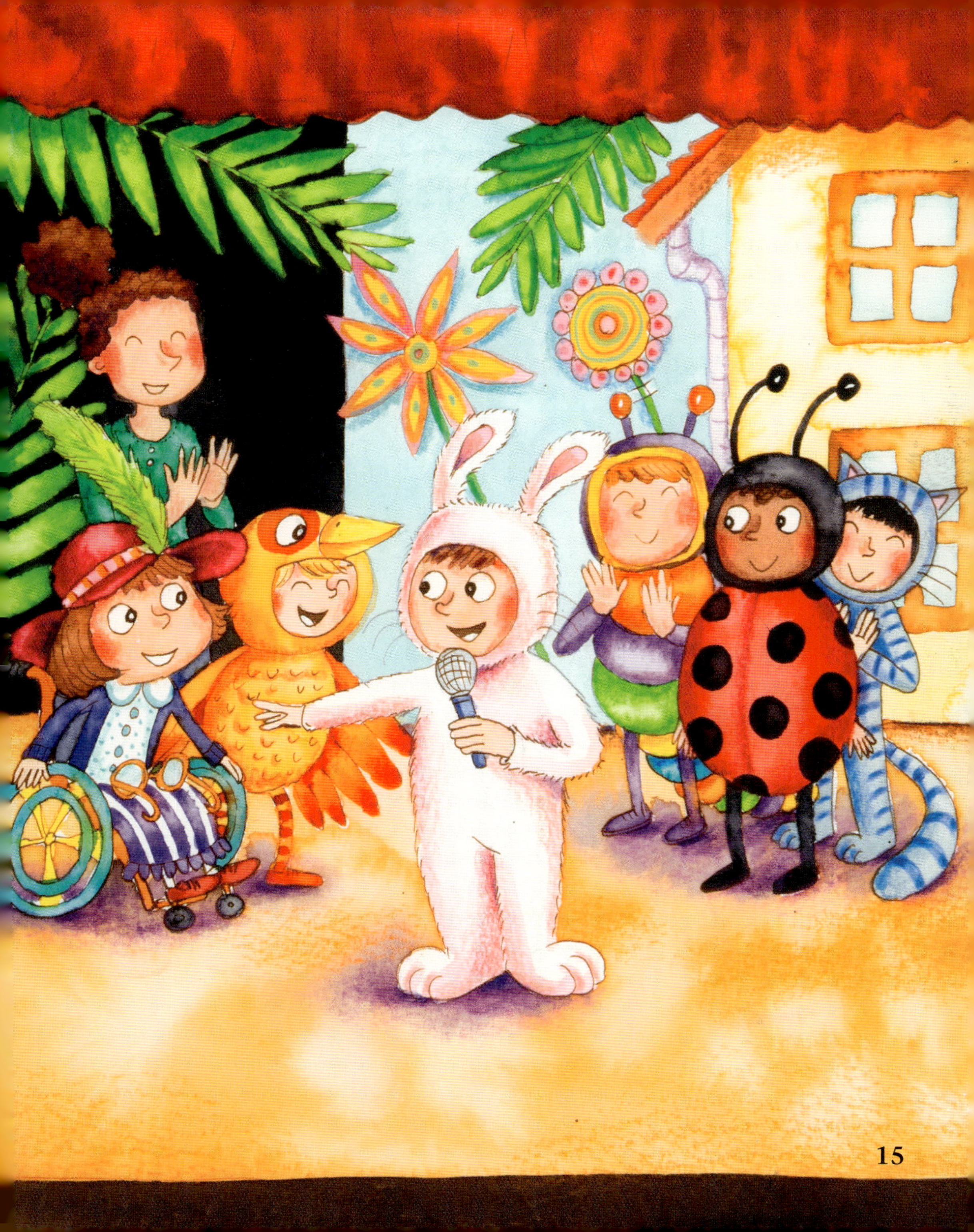

Princess looked at her friends
and gave them a big smile.
"It was the best play ever!"
she said.
"But the best part of all was …
we did the play together!"